the adventures of
TOBY
THE
GOBY

WRITTEN BY TOBY SLOUGH

ILLUSTRATED BY MICHELLE SLOUGH

THE ADVENTURES OF TOBY THE GOBY

© 2021 Toby Slough.

ISBN (Electronic Edition): 978-1-7361926-8-9

ISBN (Paperback Edition): 978-1-7361926-6-5

Printed in the United States of America

Layout and design by Michelle Slough

Published by Baldy and the Two Bears, Denton, Texas | BEAGOBY.COM

To contact the author: info@beagoby.com | www.beagoby.com

You gave me a love for books.

You taught me how to swim upstream.

You're one of the strongest people that I've ever met.

I love you Mom.

Love, Toby

There once was a
fish named Toby.

He lived in Hawaii and spent his days
splashing in the ocean with his good
friends, Willie and Ali.

Willie, the whale, swam with ease in the salty water. He was happy in the big blue ocean. He had fun teaching Toby how to be steady and strong.

Ali, the albatross, soared with strength above the salty water. She was happy by the big blue ocean. She had fun teaching Toby how to be brave and fast.

When gobies grow up, they swim up
the sparkling streams to live their most
fabulous life in the mountains.

Willie and Ali knew someday Toby
would need to swim up the stream.
Willie and Ali told him...

Toby, you are a
SPECIAL goby.
You are made
extraordinary
because of the SON.
There is nothing you
can't do. It won't be
easy. But you will
NEVER be alone.
The Son is always
with you.

You will live your most fabulous life swimming with your goby friends. You will SPLASH and SING in the bright sunlight. Do hard things. Swim upstream. Follow the Son. Be a GOBY!

Toby knew he was made for mountain top living. He knew he was created for splashing around with all kinds of friends with all kinds of fins!

But the swim up
the mountain kinda
scared him.

Toby started noticing the big
strong fins of the other goby fish.

He was jealous of how fast
they could swim. The more
he watched them, the more
extraordinary they seemed.

Some of his goby friends
had pink fins.

Some of his goby friends
had green fins.

ALL of his goby friends swam as fast as racecars.

Some gobies would look
at Toby and laugh.

They whispered and giggled
about his tiny fins and not so
strong tail.

HAHA!
HA!
HAHA!

Toby would look at his fins and sigh,
"If only my fins were pink or green,
I could swim fast too."

He started listening to what
other gobies called him.

He started believing that
he had ordinary fins. He
started believing that he
could only swim in ordinary
waves. He started believing
he would never be able to
leave the salty ocean.

His head was swimming with
many thinking thoughts!

For many nights
and many days,
Toby practiced
swimming.

He worked his
right fin.

He worked his
left fin.

He even worked
his tail fin!

Left fin...1-2-3!

Right fin...1-2-3!

Over and over.

Over and over.

Over and over.

Over and over.

Over and over.

Over and over.

Until one day, he worked
his tail fin and took off
LIKE A RACECAR!

Toby was ready to start his
swim up the fresh stream.

24

The very next morning,
as the sun peeked over
the waves, toby yawned
and stretched his fins.

He swam a warm up lap with Willie.

Ali flew above him as he made his way
to the start of the fresh water stream.

Toby began his swim upstream. He
noticed some gobies swam way up
ahead not having any trouble with
the scary logs that came their way.

Some gobies swam
by themselves.

Some gobies had trouble.

Some gobies got distracted,

Some gobies wanted to turn back.

Some gobies took their eyes off the sun.

Not Toby. Toby kept his eyes
on the sun!

He remembered the good things
Willie and Ali said about him.

His heart beat faster.
He was filled with hope.

Toby swam alongside a goby that was struggling with the strong current.

Toby said to her, "Come on, friend. Let's follow the sun! I will swim ahead and make the waters easier for you!"

They bravely made their way
past scary logs.

They kept swimming.
They kept being gobies.

As Toby swam he could feel himself get stronger.

First his left fin,

 then his right fin,

even his tail fin!

Toby could feel his heart get braver.

It was a big scary stream,
but he was making it!

He and all his goby friends
were making it!

He looked to his right and looked to his left. He saw that he was surrounded by many goby friends!

As they finally made it to the top of the mountain, he could hear in his heart in a very special voice...

Toby, you are a
SPECIAL goby.
You are made
extraordinary
because of the SON.
There is nothing you
can't do. It won't be
easy. But you will
NEVER be alone.
The Son is always
with you.

You will live your most fabulous life swimming with your goby friends. You will SPLASH and SING in the bright sunlight. Do hard things. Swim upstream. Follow the Son. Be a GOBY!

Toby and his goby friends live
their most fabulous life swimming
in and out of the sunshine,
splashing and singing.

And they never take their
eyes off the Son!

Hello Friend,

I have something very important I want to share with you.

You are not ordinary.

I know God and I know He made you on purpose and for a purpose.

Where you see a blank on the next page, insert your name and read the following passage. I pray you are reminded that God is always with you - even if you feel like he is far away. Always follow the Son. We may not understand all of His ways, but we can trust Him no matter what.

Be a Goby,
Toby

_____, you are a
SPECIAL goby.

You are made extraordinary
because of the SON. There is
nothing you can't do. It won't
be easy. But you will NEVER
be alone. The Son is always
with you. You will live your
most fabulous life swimming
with your goby friends. You will
SPLASH and SING in the bright
sunlight. Do hard things.
Swim upstream. Follow the Son!

Be a GOBY!

how-to draw TOBY

1. draw the body

2. draw the fins

3. add the details

4. add the eyes and mouth

now you try!

how-to draw ALI

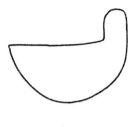

1. draw the body

2. draw the feet

3. add the wing and beak

4. add the eye and details

now you try!

how-to draw WILLIE

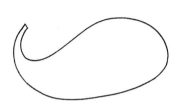

1. draw the body

2. draw the fins

3. add the eye and mouth

4. add the details

now you try!

40 I AMS

1. A Child of God
"The Spirit himself testifies with our spirit that we are God's children." - Romans 8:16

2. Safe from danger
"Let the redeemed of the Lord tell their story— those he redeemed from the hand of the foe," - Psalm 107:2

3. Forgiven
"For he has rescued us from the dominion of darkness and brought us into the kingdom of the Son he loves, in whom we have redemption, the forgiveness of sins." - Colossians 1:13-14

4. Saved by grace
"For it is by grace you have been saved, through faith—and this is not from yourselves, it is the gift of God." - Ephesians 2:8

5. Finding peace through Jesus
"Therefore, since we have been justified through faith, we have peace with God through our Lord Jesus Christ," - Romans 5:1

6. One of God's People
"To the church of God in Corinth, to those sanctified in Christ Jesus and called to be his holy people, together with all those   everywhere who call on the name of our Lord Jesus Christ—their Lord and ours:" - 1 Corinthians 1:2

7. A new creation
"Therefore, if anyone is in Christ, the new creation has come: The old has gone, the new is here!" - 2 Corinthians 5:17

8. Invited to God's promises
"Through these he has given us his very great and precious promises, so that through them you may participate in the divine   nature, having escaped the corruption in the world caused by evil desires."
- 2 Peter 1:4

9. Free and full of grace

Christ redeemed us from the curse of the law by becoming a curse for us, for it is written: "Cursed is everyone who is hung on a pole." - Galatians 3:13

10. Living in God's Kingdom

"For he has rescued us from the dominion of darkness and brought us into the kingdom of the Son he loves," - Colossians 1:13

11. Led by the Spirit of God

"For those who are led by the Spirit of God are the children of God." - Romans 8:14

12. One of God's kids

"For those who are led by the Spirit of God are the children of God." - Romans 8:14

13. Safe in God

"For he will command his angels concerning you to guard you in all your ways; - Psalm 91:11

14. Getting all my needs met by Jesus

"And my God will meet all your needs according to the riches of his glory in Christ Jesus."
- Philippians 4:19

15. Giving all my worries to Jesus

" Cast all your anxiety on him because he cares for you." - 1 Peter 5:7

16. Strong in Christ

"Finally, be strong in the Lord and in his mighty power." - 1 Ephesians 6:10

17. Doing all things through Christ

"I can do all this through him who gives me strength." - Philippians 4:13

18. Sharing glory with God

"Now if we are children, then we are heirs—heirs of God and co-heirs with Christ, if indeed we share in his sufferings in order that we may also share in his glory."
- Romans 8:17

19. Blessed like Abraham

"Christ redeemed us from the curse of the law by becoming a curse for us, for it is written: "Cursed is everyone who is hung on a pole." He redeemed us in order that the blessing given to Abraham might come to the Gentiles through Christ Jesus, so that by faith we might receive the promise of the Spirit."
Galatians 3:13-14

20. Observing and doing what God asks

"The Lord will open the heavens, the storehouse of his bounty, to send rain on your land in season and to bless all the work of your hands. You will lend to many nations but will borrow from none." - Deuteronomy 28:12

21. Blessed, blessed, blessed

"You will be blessed when you come in and blessed when you go out."
- Deuteronomy 28:6

22. Finding my life in Jesus

"And this is the testimony: God has given us eternal life, and this life is in his Son. Whoever has the Son has life; whoever does not have the Son of God does not have life." - 1 John 5:11-12

23. Blessed by God

"Praise be to the God and Father of our Lord Jesus Christ, who has blessed us in the heavenly realms with every spiritual blessing in Christ." - Ephesians 1:3

24. Healed by Jesus

"He himself bore our sins" in his body on the cross, so that we might die to sins and live for righteousness; "by his wounds you have been healed." - 1 Peter 2:24

25. Safe and protected

"I have given you authority to trample on snakes and scorpions and to overcome all the power of the enemy; nothing will harm you." - Luke 10:19

26. First not last

"The Lord will make you the head, not the tail. If you pay attention to the commands of the Lord your God that I give you this day and carefully follow them, you will always be at the top, never at the bottom." - Deuteronomy 28:13

27. A conqueror
"No, in all these things we are more than conquerors through him who loved us." - Romans 8:37

28. Full of God's power
"I will give you the keys of the kingdom of heaven; whatever you bind on earth will be[a] bound in heaven, and whatever you loose on earth will be[b] loosed in heaven." - Matthew 16:19

29. An overcomer
"They triumphed over him by the blood of the Lamb and by the word of their testimony; they did not love their lives so much as to shrink from death." - Revelation 12:11

30. Living with God inside of me
"You, dear children, are from God and have overcome them, because the one who is in you is greater than the one who is in the world." - 1 John 4:4

31. Keeping my eyes on Jesus
"So we fix our eyes not on what is seen, but on what is unseen, since what is seen is temporary, but what is unseen is eternal. - 2 Corinthians 4:18

32. Walking by faith
"For we live by faith, not by sight." - 2 Corinthians 5:7

33. Fighting like Jesus
The weapons we fight with are not the weapons of the world. On the contrary, they have divine power to demolish strongholds. We demolish arguments and every pretension that sets itself up against the knowledge of God, and we take captive every thought to make it obedient to Christ. -
- 2 Corinthians 10:4-5

34. Learning to think like God
"We demolish arguments and every pretension that sets itself up against the knowledge of God, and we take captive every thought to make it obedient to Christ." - 2 Corinthians 10:5

35. Changed by what I think

"Therefore, I urge you, brothers and sisters, in view of God's mercy, to offer your bodies as a living sacrifice, holy and pleasing to God—this is your true and proper worship. Do not conform to the pattern of this world but be transformed by the renewing of your mind. Then you will be able to test and approve what God's will is—his good, pleasing and perfect will." - Romans 12:1-2

36. God's partner

"For we are co-workers in God's service; you are God's field, God's building."
- 1 Corinthians 3:9

37. In Christ

"God made him who had no sin to be sin[a] for us, so that in him we might become the righteousness of God." - 2 Corinthians 5:21

38. Living like Christ

"Follow God's example, therefore, as dearly loved children" - Ephesians 5:1

39. The light of the world

"You are the salt of the earth. But if the salt loses its saltiness, how can it be made salty again? It is no longer good for anything, except to be thrown out and trampled underfoot. You are the light of the world. A town built on a hill cannot be hidden."
- Matthew 5:13-14

40. Blessing and praising Jesus with my life

"I will extol the Lord at all times; his praise will always be on my lips." - Psalm 34:1

SCRIPTURE REFERENCES

Romans 12:2
Do not conform to the pattern of this world, but be transformed by the renewing of your mind. Then you will be able to test and approve what God's will is—his good, pleasing and perfect will.

Hebrews 12:1-3
Therefore, since we are surrounded by such a great cloud of witnesses, let us throw off everything that hinders and the sin that so easily entangles. And let us run with perseverance the race marked out for us, fixing our eyes on Jesus, the pioneer and perfecter of faith. For the joy set before him he endured the cross, scorning its shame, and sat down at the right hand of the throne of God. Consider him who endured such opposition from sinners, so that you will not grow weary and lose heart.

Matthew 5:16
In the same way, let your light shine before others, that they may see your good deeds and glorify your Father in heaven.

Psalm 139:14
I praise you because I am fearfully and wonderfully made; your works are wonderful, I know that full well.

Pslam 27:13-14
I remain confident of this: I will see the goodness of the Lord in the land of the living. Wait for the Lord; be strong and take heart and wait for the Lord.

Romans 12:1
Therefore, I urge you, brothers and sisters, in view of God's mercy, to offer your bodies as a living sacrifice, holy and pleasing to God—this is your true and proper worship.

1 Corinthians 2:16
"Who has known the mind of the Lord so as to instruct him?" But we have the mind of Christ."

ABOUT THE AUTHOR

After graduating from Abilene Christian University in 1986, Toby began his ministry career in San Antonio, Texas, working with high school students. During his youth ministry years, Toby traveled around the country speaking to teenagers and youth leaders. In 2000, Toby and his wife Mika, along with twelve other families began Cross Timbers Church in the back of a bar. The idea for Cross Timbers was birthed from a calling God gave Toby to plant a church for hurting and broken people. For more than twenty years, God has been building, shaping, and refining the cornerstone foundations at Cross Timbers.

Toby and Mika have been married for over thirty-four years. He often says he married way over his head. Toby and Mika have a daughter Bailey-she, and her husband Grant have three kids, Gideon, Micah, and Esther. Toby and Mika's son, Ross, and his wife Michelle have two daughters June and Evie. His family brings him more joy than any one man could ever ask for. In his free time, Toby enjoys cooking, reading, writing, and gardening.

Toby serves as the Lead Pastor for Cross Timbers. Toby has authored several books including, *Not Yet*, *Living the Dream*, *The Great Adventure*, *God Drives Me Crazy*, *Normal*, *It Is Well*, **and** *Harvest*.

You can follow Toby on Twitter: @tobyslough
Or find him on Facebook: www.facebook.com/tobyslough

ABOUT THE ILLUSTRATOR

Michelle Slough is a wife, mother, and graphic designer based in Denton, Texas. She and her husband Ross have two spirited daughters, Everly (5) and June (2). She illustrated this book from a unique perspective, knowing she would be reading it with her own littles in her lap.

Since Michelle was a young child, she loved all things art and drawing. It has been a lifelong goal and dream of hers to illustrate a children's book. Her most recent projects include illustration and design work for Finn + Emma, Blessed is She, Cross Timbers Church and more.